SHARP
REFLECTIONS

EDWIN LE GRICE

First published in 1993 by
KEVIN MAYHEW LTD
Rattlesden
Bury St Edmunds
Suffolk IP30 0SZ

Acknowledgements
The publishers wish to express their gratitude
to the following for permission to use copyright material:

Cambridge University Press for extracts from the
Authorised Version of the Bible (The King James Bible),
the rights in which are vested in the Crown,
and reproduced by permission of the Crown's patentee.

Hodder & Stoughton Ltd for extracts from the
Holy Bible, New International Version.
Copyright 1973, 1978, 1984 by International Bible Society.
All rights reserved.

The Division of Christian Education of the National Council
of the Churches of Christ in the USA for extracts from the
New Revised Standard Version of the Bible, copyright 1989.

Front cover: Photo © Heather Angel.
Reproduced by kind permission.

ISBN   0 86209 432 1

Cover design by Graham Johnstone
Typesetting and Page Creation by Anne Haskell
Printed and bound in Great Britain.

Contents

Credo

Biography of Edwin Le Grice

Edwin Le Grice spent his early years in a farming and fishing community in Norfolk.

At Cambridge he changed from Mathematics to Theology, which explains his respect for both disciplines. It is possible that he regarded Mathematics as the language of the universe!

After living in the country, he chose at first to work in the industrial city of Leeds. Over thirty years his work took him and his family in an almost complete circle: Devon, London, St Albans and finally to become Dean of Ripon, working in the Cathedral where he was ordained thirty-five years earlier.

He became a Church Commissioner, a Member of General Synod and the Crown Appointments Commission, all of which rather surprised him.

Ripon, its Cathedral and people gave him great delight. He did not find faith easy. He was still exploring and tried to express his experience in a new found ability in retirement to write poetry.

Edwin Le Grice also wrote the text for the Cantata – *Love Unknown*, (Mayhew, 1992).

Publisher's Note

Most of the poems in this collection were originally written as reflections upon biblical passages under the title, *Sharp Reflections*, and are presented here in that form. However, six additional poems have been added, three in the first section, and three in the third. For devotional use, these have been paired with biblical passages. In the case of *Relativity*, it was clearly the author's intention that this should stand on its own, and this has been respected.

Another change from the original presentation is in the use of different translations of the bible. In one or two cases the original Authorised Version text has been retained, while the rest have been replaced with either the New Revised Standard Version or the New International Version.

Preface

The thinking Christian has much in common with the enquiring agnostic.

On the one hand are the people who know the answers and can tell you with enviable assurance what you should or should not believe. Some of them are fundamentalists, some atheists.

In the middle are those who are acutely aware that to many of life's most important questions they do not know the answers. Some are agnostic in the text-book sense of not believing it possible ever to know; but the other agnostics (Christian or otherwise) are like Abraham 'seeking a country', or Columbus refusing to turn back to Europe. Their refusal to give up the search is not far, I believe, from what the Bible calls 'faith'. And honesty is one of its essential ingredients.

The scientific method is certainly one approach to truth – but not the only one. The Beethoven Ninth Symphony, like a great deal of art and poetry, can give us an insight into life's meaning perhaps more significant than any scientific treatise.

For this reason I believe it is important to remember that the language of religion – of Scripture and Creeds and Liturgy – is poetry rather than prose: it conveys more than it states. The meditations in this book do not attempt to take the scriptures literally, but to reflect upon them – I hope poetically and honestly.

EDWIN LE GRICE

For Betty

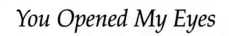

You Opened My Eyes

*He answered, '. . . One thing I know, that though I was blind,
now I see.'*

JOHN 9:25

YOU OPENED MY EYES

Not that I was blind:
You showed me where to look.
Herb-Robert first, then green-flowered spurge,
Stitchwort, crosswort, wind-flowers, avens of dusty brown,
And on and on and on it's gone
Eyes slowly opening to unexpected joy.

Not that I could not see.
The flowers arranged so delicately, so subtly on my desk
Would stay for hours unnoticed
Till suddenly, prompted perhaps by you
My eyes at last would focus on them
And then I'd see
See more and more and go on seeing.

Not only flowers –
North Sea cormorants disappearing, emerging,
Drying black shaggy wings on island rocks,
Oyster catchers flashing black and white semaphore beside
                                        a Scottish loch,
Dippers with quick nervous nodding nesting beside the Swale,
Barn-owl with soft hushed flight, puffed plump plumage
Reluctant eyes sleepily so wide wide open
As slowly you opened mine.

You opened my ears
Not that I was deaf
But together we learnt to listen –
Barbarolli, Solomon, Hamilton Harty, Myra Hess,
Sitting hard behind the orchestra on Town Hall floor
Ten feet from tympani; not many more from bliss;
Doors opening into heaven:

To poetry too –
I'd just discovered Hopkins,
His other-worldly worldliness, sensuous spirituality,
The subtle springing of his rhythm:
You widened my range, lengthened the waves of my reception,
Made me hear Marvell, Donne, the poem-prayers of Andrewes:
From Wordsworth, Keats and Coleridge to Flecker, Yeats
And the S.O.S. distress of Sylvia Plath
You opened my ears.

You opened my heart –
But you know all about that.

The kingdom of heaven is like treasure hidden in a field. When a man found it, he hid it again, and then in his joy went and sold all he had and bought that field.

Again, the kingdom of heaven is like a merchant looking for fine pearls.

When he found one of great value, he went away and sold everything he had and bought it.

MATTHEW 13:44-46

HIDDEN TREASURE

Subtleties of truth
How can mere words imprison what they are?
Only the poet from within
Can glimpse or share that star

Truth's oyster keeps its treasure locked
Prised open you may spy it
Not all the pearls of wisdom you can sell
Will yield enough to buy it

The truth is camouflaged
Identity and whereabouts concealed
Hazard the savings of a life-time's dreams
To buy that field.

The king sent again a captain of the third fifty with his fifty.

And the third captain of the fifty went up, and came and fell on his knees before Elijah, and besought him, and said unto him, 'O man of God, I pray thee, let my life and the life of these fifty thy servants, be precious in thy sight.'

Behold, there came fire down from heaven, and burnt up the two captains of the former fifties with their fifties; therefore let my life now be precious in thy sight.

And the angel of the Lord said unto Elijah, 'Go down with him: be not afraid of him.' And he arose, and went down with him unto the king.

2 KINGS 1:13-15

And the Samaritans did not receive him, becuase his face was as though he would go to Jerusalem.

And when his disciples James and John saw this, they said, 'Lord, wilt thou that we command fire to come down from heaven, and consume them, even as Elias did?'

But he turned, and rebuked them, and said, 'Ye know not what manner of spirit ye are of.'

For the Son of man is not come to destroy men's lives, but to save them. And they went to another village.

LUKE 9:53-56

NUCLEAR ANNIVERSARY

You would think twice would be enough
Two captains with their fifties
Obliterated in a moment
Cascade of fire from heaven
Elijah's fearful trembling touch upon the button.
What kind of cloud was that hanging above the hill
Where the prophet sat in judgement?
You would think twice would be enough.

Was it deterring fear – of God or of destruction,
Was it humility or even prayer which broke the vicious circle?
Or were all three involved?
The human race consumes so easily –
Wonderful fodder for the fire from heaven.
In whose sight, whose searching sight, are our lives precious?

Another fear it was, fear in the prophet's heart which
                              triggered off destruction;
Repeated fear, until the angelic intervention.
'Don't be afraid of him, he is your brother,
His life is precious.'

You would think twice would be enough –
Hiroshima and Nagasaki.
Will fear, humility or prayer break this vicious circle?
The whole world's history, accumulated achievement,
Millions of beating hearts, creative minds,
In whose sight are they precious?
What cloud hangs over us?
What manner of spirit are we of?
You would think twice would be enough.

Woe to the bloody city! It is all full of lies and robbery.

And it shall come to pass, that all they that look upon thee shall flee from thee, and say, 'Ninevah is laid waste: who will bemoan her? Whence shall I seek comforters for thee?'

NAHUM 3:1,7

Then Jonah went out of the city and sat down east of the city, and made a booth for himself there. He sat under it in the shade, waiting to see what would become of the city.

Then the Lord said, 'And should I not be concerned about Nineveh, that great city, in which there are more than a hundred and twenty thousand persons who do not know their right hand from their left, and also many animals?'

JONAH 4:5,11

EVIL EMPIRE

'Take away my life' cries Jonah,
Worm-eaten fragments of his cherished gourd,
His mushroom-shield from solar radiation
Scattered around his booth –
'Take away my life:

'How can I live in the same world as Nineveh?'
And silhouetted on the sky-line there stands the city
Forty days ultimatum now expired
Undemolished, undestroyed, outlined against the lurid
                              threatening of the rising sun –
There in the trembling image of its scorching heat:
Red squares, spires, minarets and domes:
'Take away my life: what is there left to live for?'

'But Jonah,
Consider Nineveh, that great city,
Filled with accumulated treasures of its rich inheritance:
Look at its people, more than six score thousand
Artisans and artists, poets, politicians not discriminating
                              left from right:
Consider the cattle, sharing the sack-cloth and ashes
                              of humanity,
Breathing the same air, drinking the same water, threatened
                              by the same destruction:

'Jonah,
If you have pity on yourself and on your perished gourd,
Should not I have pity
On the bloody city?'

And Moses took the calf they had made and burned it in the fire; then he ground it to powder, scattered it on the water and made the Israelites drink it.

He said to Aaron, 'What did these people do to you, that you led them into such great sin?'

'Do not be angry, my lord,' Aaron answered. 'You know how prone these people are to evil.

They said to me, "Make us gods who will go before us. As for this fellow Moses who brought us up out of Egypt, we don't know what has happened to him."

So I told them, "Whoever has any gold jewellery, take it off." Then they gave me the gold, and I threw it into the fire, and out came this calf!'

EXODUS 32:20-24

OUT CAME THIS CALF

'Out came this calf' said Aaron guilelessly,
'I only collected the jewels –
Gold and silver the people gave me . . .
Not even my own treasures,
Nothing original about them,
Ultimately everything in life is second-hand.

'I just wandered about with an open box
And willingly they gave me what they had:
Rings for fingers, ears and noses,
Necklaces of silver-gilt filigree,
Bracelets, single, double, multiple, criss-crossing
Covering, enhancing the softness of the arm right to the elbow:
There was even a coronet!

'The people gave them to me:
I just dropped them in –
Into the scorching ferment of the cauldron
Where spirit mingles and compounds with matter,
– And out came this calf!'

'Oh no!', he cried, 'Of course it isn't Yahweh!
I know we mustn't worship it.
But in the absence of anything better
Won't it lead us, can't it lead us
To our promised land?'

And he wept disconsolate
When Moses made him tear it up,
Destroy it,
Grind it into powder,
Drink it down,
And live forever with the taste of his failed vision.

When the woman saw that the fruit of the tree was good for food and pleasing to the eye, and also desirable for gaining wisdom, she took some and ate it. She also gave some to her husband, who was with her, and he ate it.

Then the eyes of both of them were opened, and they realized they were naked; so they sewed fig leaves together and made coverings for themselves.

GENESIS 3:6-7

O sov'reign, virtuous, precious of all trees in Paradise . . .
. . . Henceforth my early care,
Not without song, each morning and due praise,
Shall tend thee and the fertile burden ease
Of thy full branches offer'd free to all;
Till dieted by thee, I grow mature
In knowledge, as the gods who all things know.

Much pleasure we have lost, while we abstain'd
From this delightful fruit, nor know till now
True relish, tasting: if such pleasure be
In things to us forbidden, it might be wish'd
For this one tree had been forbidden ten.

JOHN MILTON, *PARADISE LOST*, Book IX

TEN TREES

Paradise in Yorkshire?
No Lucifer has leapt this crumbling dry-stone mill-stone
                                    lime-stone boundary wall
This blissful bower violets underfoot
Late primrose still in flower
Even an aven here and there in May
And blue-bells everywhere ringing their changing shades
In pale and deep confusion. Pink among blue
Orchids in profusion pattern the grassy floor
With Milton's rich inlay.
Beechbuds have burst their light-brown paper shells
Flocks of their crisp new fledgling leaves of lucent green
Fly in the sunshine high
Pattern'd in network of the finest lace
Slenderest stems delicately tenderly holding them in place
Against a sky pale blue-bell blue above
Paler still below where flush from evening sun
Tinges the distant wood with orchid blush
No knowledge here of ill
No fruit proffered forbidden still
But freely offered and for all
Anticipation delectation with spring-time promise and no
                                    cause for trepidation

Beauty not of one tree alone
But Adam's longed for ten –
After the fall.

She brought forth her firstborn son, and wrapped him in swaddling clothes, and laid him in a manger; because there was no room for them in the inn.

And there were in the same country shepherds.

LUKE 2:7,8

STABLE BIRTH

The first lambs come at Christmas

Waking to wildness of this wintry night
I see through opened mullioned cottage window
The moon motionless
Holding her own against the stream
Of jostling joyous crowds
Of dark bright-edged eager excited clouds
Spilling into the courtyard farmyard
Fitful fleeting flashes
Bright floods and splashes
Of cold reflected gold and silver light

I smell from the dark dank stable
Sudden pungency of mingled straw and dung

And between creaking shrieking moaning groaning of the wind
And pitiful crying of a ewe
Hear quick firm footsteps of the farmer's wife
Crossing the hard cobbles of the yard
Bringing skilled country midwifery
To save new life.

It's a hard season to be born
For lamb
A cold rough place
For man.

And why do you worry about clothes? See how the lilies of the field grow. They do not labour or spin.

Yet I tell you that not even Solomon in all his splendour was dressed like one of these.

If that is how God clothes the grass of the field, which is here today and tomorrow is thrown into the fire, will he not much more clothe you, O you of little faith?

MATTHEW 6:28-30

The Queen of Sheba said to the king, 'The report I heard in my own country about your achievements and your wisdom is true.

But I did not believe these things until I came and saw with my own eyes. Indeed, not even half was told me; in wisdom and wealth you have far exceeded the report I heard.'

1 KINGS 10:6-7

And Solomon had seven hundred wives, princesses, and three hundred concubines.

1 KINGS 11:3

A CONSIDERATION OF LILIES

Consider those lovely Lent lilies
Stretching mile upon mile beside long lonely mountains
Picos de Europa, nothing in Europe like them
Glimpses of snow streaks
Lightest of pale sky, darkest of blue grey nimbus
And everywhere those lilies to consider.

Not much comfort you'll get from it
Little encouragement to share their jocundity
Their short lives, their substance squandered on the desert air
One way or another they are all for the oven
Their passing away so soon, is it no cause for tears?

And you?
For no consideration can you claim immunity
No mutual assurance for love's security
No limits to its liability
All go the same way.

But look around you
What extravagance of grace
What generosity unbonded, unbounded
Prodigious prodigality
Felicitous fecundity
Squandering of resources
Lovely unlasting illumination
Life blazing at both ends
Not even Solomon in all his glory
With seven hundred wives, three hundred concubines
Could hold a candle.

If I give all I possess to the poor and surrender my body to the flames, but if I have not love, I gain nothing.

I Corinthians 13:3

The next day he took out two silver coins and gave them to the innkeeper. 'Look after him,' he said, 'and when I return, I will reimburse you for any extra expense you may have.'

Luke 10:35

EROS AND AGAPE

Love is not feeling, so they tell us,
Love is not liking;
Love is above such things, aloof, aloft,
Eros and Agape stand wide apart –
But do they?

Love is not deeds, Saint Paul insists:
Feeding the hungry, the martyred body burnt:
Not even social service – the oil, the wine, two
                                    proffered pence –
All can be worthless.
But can they?

Or is love both?
Heart drawn to heart, hand stretched to hand,
A sacrament of touch,
Conscious, deliberate step towards the brink with full intent,
Liking, compassion, caring, serving –
And then the plunge, out of control,
The fall of man,
Dreadful descent into the arms of God,
Falling – in love . . .

But I tell you, Do not resist an evil person. If someone strikes you on the right cheek, turn to him the other also.

MATTHEW 5:39

On the contrary: 'If your enemy is hungry, feed him; if he is thirsty, give him something to drink. In doing this, you will heap burning coals on his head.'

ROMANS 12:20

These men were bound in their coats, their hosen, and their hats, and their other garments, and were cast into the midst of the burning fiery furnace.

And the princes, governors, and captains, and the king's counsellors, being gathered together, saw these men, upon whose bodies the fire had no power, nor was an hair of their head singed, neither were their coats changed, nor the smell of fire had passed on them.

DANIEL 3:21,27

THE OTHER CHEEK

The first cheek politely proffered
Kissed with formal courtesy
Lips scarcely sensing
Delicate smoothness of complexion.

But the second offered
With lightest slightest suggestion
Of seduction

Nothing
Is more provocative
Than turning the other cheek

The first rudely struck
Bruised texture
Flushed surface reflecting
Striker's cruel anger

The second presented
In meekness
Or masochism

Is sticking your neck out
A necessary concomitant
Of turning the other cheek?

Bound in their coats and hosen
Their hats and other garments
Cast into burning fiery furnace
Shadrach Meshach and Abednego
Walked around unharmed
Cheerfully singing the Benedicite
Not a hair singed
No smell of fire passed on them

But the flames which set them free
Cast down and utterly consumed
The hapless stokers

Hungry
Feed your enemy
Thirsty
Give him drink
Heap coals of fire
On his hatless head

Nothing
Is more provocative
Than turning the other cheek.

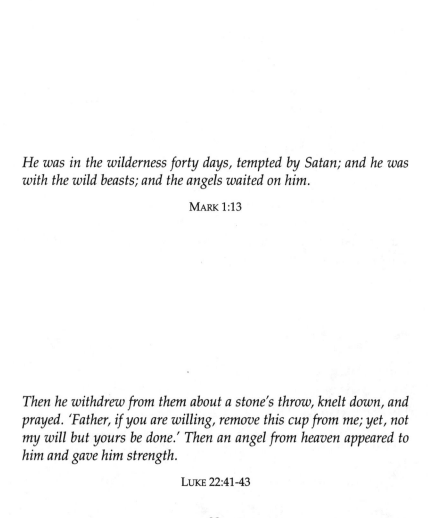

He was in the wilderness forty days, tempted by Satan; and he was with the wild beasts; and the angels waited on him.

MARK 1:13

Then he withdrew from them about a stone's throw, knelt down, and prayed. 'Father, if you are willing, remove this cup from me; yet, not my will but yours be done.' Then an angel from heaven appeared to him and gave him strength.

LUKE 22:41-43

ANGELIC CHORUS

Bright angel hosts who serve in realms above
Your glorious wings display:
Break through the clouds which veil God's heart of love:
Reveal creation's day.

You marshalled forces of the powers of right
Your ordered ranks deploy
To pierce the evil armour of hell's might
With shafts of heavenly joy.

O morning stars who hailed a new world's birth,
With shouts of praise acclaim
Beyond the unfolding wonders of the earth
The glory of his name.

Amid the desert's terrors forty days
Or in the Garden's night
Surround us with your symphony of praise,
God's messengers of light.

Then some of the Pharisees and teachers of the law said to him, 'Teacher, we want to see a miraculous sign from you.'

He answered, 'A wicked and adulterous generation asks for a miraculous sign! But none will be given it except the sign of the prophet Jonah.

For as Jonah was three days and three nights in the belly of a huge fish, so the Son of Man will be three days and three nights in the heart of the earth.

The men of Nineveh will stand up at the judgment with this generation and condemn it; for they repented at the preaching of Jonah, and now one greater than Jonah is here.'

MATTHEW 12: 38-41

SPITTING IMAGE

What daring:
Comparing
Jesus with Jonah.

Down in the ship's sides
Or on a pillow in the hinder part
Asleep
In the deep:

Until the cry,
'What do you mean, sleeper?'
'Don't you care if we die?'
'Crucify! Crucify!'

After three days,
As the scriptures tell,
Wonderfully ejected –
Thrown up
From the belly
Of hell.

Scarecrow figure
Outside the city wall
Screaming vengeance:
Spitting image to recall
One nailed like vermin on the farmyard gate
Spread-eagled there in dying pain
Praying forgiveness:

Does it take this
To make us think again?

When Paul had said this, he knelt down with all of them and prayed.

They all wept as they embraced him and kissed him.

What grieved them most was his statement that they would never see his face again. Then they accompanied him to the ship.

After we had torn ourselves away from them, we put out to sea and sailed straight to Cos. The next day we went to Rhodes and from there to Patara.

We found a ship crossing over to Phoenicia, went on board and set sail.

Acts 20:36-38; 21:1-2

DREAMING OF PAUL AT PATARA

Patara
Lying here lazily drowsily
Blue Aegean, dazzling sun, sand too hot for bare feet
White waves of dunes smothering swamping the living
                                        stirring past
Flotsam of ruins
Ionic sculpture, Greek inscriptions, obelisks, sarcophogi,
Even a legendary light-house.

Forest frame of undulating pines
Opening, shutting rich dark green umbrellas
Shielding, shading brown, red, purple soil
Splodged, splashed with pink of oleander,
Crimsoned pomegranate,
And everywhere the warm and subtle scent of thyme:

Bamboo-edged sky-reflecting river
Splashing its placid course from Xanthos to the sea,
Watering a verdant valley:
And in blue distance,
Snow-slashed shoulders of threatening herds of
                                        Taurus mountains.

Fresh in our minds the memory of Xanthos
Like a tall thin minaret
Its delicately coloured pencil-point piercing the skin of time,
Letting the past seep through:
Its silence like the muezzin's cry
Ascending, descending the steps, half-steps, quarter-steps
                                                of tone
In oriental cadence
As we sensed the warmth of thousands of arena seats
Pictured assembling crowds scrambling the steps, half-steps,
                                        quarter-steps of stone
Glimpsed surviving ruins of houses, baths, brothels, temple,
                                                churches,
Protruding from obliterating swamps of history.

And here at Patara
Dreaming in sunshine,
Paul's ship sails straight over us
Splashing aside hot waves of smothering sand;
Hand on his shaven head,
Myopic eyes peering in thorn-pierced pain,
Fearless of bonds, imprisonment or death,
Mind full of Ephesus, Troas, Miletus,
Heart set on Rome:

Pursuing his course with joy.

Jesus said to her, 'Do not hold on to me, because I have not yet ascended to the Father. But go to my brothers and say to them, 'I am ascending to my Father and your Father, to my God and your God,' Mary Magdalene went and announced to the disciples. 'I have seen the Lord'; and she told them that he had said these things to her.

JOHN 20:17-18

STRID

You cannot hold the present.
Each year, day, minute, fraction of a second
Splits neatly into two – before and after:
And where between those creviced crevasse walls
You thought to grasp the present moment,
Smooth, elusive as the swift flowing surface of the Wharfe
It slips between the future's tangent and the parabolic past –
Evades you to infinity,
Avoids you to eternity.

How then each day a thousand times
Do you so lightly leap time's Strid
From then to when
Without encountering now?

And if you fell
Would it be heaven or hell?

Whenever you enter a town and its people welcome you, eat what is set before you; cure the sick who are there, and say to them, 'The kingdom of God has come near to you.'

LUKE 10:8-9

Freely ye have received; freely give.

MATTHEW 10:8

TALISMAN OF GRACE

What happiness
Beyond believing!
Stretching out arms
Wide-spread fingers, open palms,
Simply receiving –

Earth and sky in richest vesture,
Sunshine, clouds, flowers,
Beauty of form and gesture:
Love that is ours
Given without reserve:
No need to earn or to deserve,
No implication
Of any obligation
To repay some other day,
But just a simple take-away:

The subtle craft of grace! –
Conscript companion's cheerful face,
And happy smile,
Walking beside us a further weary mile.

And to crown all,
– Talisman beyond our making –
By thankfully taking
Gifts beyond recall
We freely offer others the greatest happiness of living –
The joy of giving.

In the beginning, GOD . . .

GENESIS 1:1

PRIME

Not prim but prime and full of grace:
Not celibacy but tender delicacy:
The gently curving stem, happily lifted face,
Pale yellow petals tenderly released
From firm embrace of light green sepals,
Tightly creased
Not with the complicated origami of the summer,
But with the cool simplicity of spring:
In all the glade there is no treasure
Subtly displayed to give such pleasure
As the gentle rose I bring.

Not first but prime the cause of all that is:
Whether the first great bang
Across distance of non-existence rang
To call the world to birth
And in due course our earth –
Or in mystery of cosmic history
Everything always WAS:
From nebula to universe,
Then in reverse
Matter and energy lost, but at no cosmic cost,
In some black hole: only to reappear
In a new stratosphere,
And so, whether in time or space
To take its place
In continuity of perpetuity.

Primrose or universe,
Great or small:
Instantaneous cataclysmic creation
Or spontaneous eternal generation –
Either way the cause of all
Must be of logical not temporal necessity:
Outside the reach of space and time:
Not first, but prime.

As for the earth, out of it comes bread; but underneath it is turned up as by fire.

Its stones are the place of sapphires, and its dust contains gold.

'That path no bird of prey knows, and the falcon's eye has not seen it.

The proud wild animals have not trodden it; the lion has not passed over it.

Man cuts out channels in the rocks, and his eye sees every precious thing.

But where shall wisdom be found? And where is the place of understanding?'

JOB 28:5-8, 10, 12

FINDING FOUNTAINS

Quiet grace, beauty of slender piers, ribs, vaults, broken arches:
Delicate fusion of cold grey limestone with warm
                                        stored sunshine,
Partly reflected from adzed chiselled surfaces,
Partly refracted from past ages geological,
                                        archeological, mystical.

This is the mouth of our cave:
Here the adventure began.
We came not as artists, architects, tourists, or even pilgrims,
But trained explorers, athletic ascetics,
Skilled at our task, equipment tried, tested,
Glimpsing a narrow way, a cold wet chasm,
Lured by limestone labyrinths.

Our cave was our refuge:
Here we survived while hurricanes of war and heresy
                                        scoured the land above,
Devastating, destroying the heritage of centuries of faith
                                        and culture:
Landmarks stripped, swamped: hallmarks obliterated:
We escaped extinction in speleological isolation.

It was more than survival,
More than preservation, conservation, restoration:
Banished from the wide world outside,
Splashing, squeezing our way through tunnels, channels
                                        of austerity,
We opened up, explored, a rich new universe below, within,
Extracting from forbidding seams
Sources of energy, treasures of beauty unseen before.

Lost, confused, bewildered by darkness,
Our crude torches glimmered, glowed, flared, blazed gloriously,
Revealing caverns, palaces, temples,
Sights invisible in the hard brightness of daylight,
Sounds inaudible in un-echoing space:
Stalagmites of faith, endeavour, aspiration,
Stalactites of grace, inspiration, contemplation:
In nakedness, isolation, desolation,
We stood open-mouthed, open-minded, open-hearted,
Lost in wonder, adoration:
Our cave was larger than the world outside.

When storms, floods abated, slowly we returned,
Spread patterns of disciplined activity over deserts outside:
Shared our triple economy, learned in austerity –
Controlled authority, sparse simplicity, chaste community:
Fountains, rivers of life, for field, farm, factory,
In us the world outside found strength to breathe, wake,
                                                    live again.
Flower in renaissance.

Yes we were driven out, this place a ruin, a skeleton –
Or is it broken egg-shell?
Life formed, nurtured here, has taken wings, escaped.

But you, have you destroyed our landmarks,
Rooted out hedgerows, torn up fences, hewn down forests?
When storms break – spiritual, cultural, nuclear –
Making your civilisation, technology, culture, a dust-bowl,
Where will you find fountains?

Unloved Leah

The children struggled together within her; and Rebekah said, 'If it is to be this way, why do I live?'

So she went to inquire of the Lord. And the Lord said to her, 'Two nations are in your womb, and two peoples, born of you, shall be divided; the one shall be stronger than the other, the elder shall serve the younger.'

When her time to give birth was at hand, there were twins in her womb.

The first came out red, all his body like a hairy mantle; so they named him Esau.

Afterward his brother came out, with his hand gripping Esau's heel; so he was named Jacob.

GENESIS 25:22-26

TWO NATIONS

Fearful flash-back fantasy of struggle within their
                                    mother's womb:
The blond and sleek; the red and hairy;
Smooth man of the plains and fields;
Wild man of the hills and woods;
Farmer; nomad:
Settler; explorer:

Athletic skill, gymnastic strength,
Pulsing of the blood, the chase, the kill,
Cold quick plunge in mountain pool,
Smell of the forest:

Wafting culinary scent of subtly seasoned sod of pottage,
Quiet sun-dial-ordered life, daily routine of cattle care,
Spacious tents curtained with richly coloured
                                    myriad-knotted carpets,
Cossetted, cushioned against scorch of sun or cruel
                                    bite of frost,
Civilisation, domestication, sophistication,
The song, the feast, the dance –

Yet surging uncontrollably within him,
Tides of fierce love and hate:
His hand for dear life holding on to, holding back
His brother's heel.

When the Lord saw that Leah was unloved, he opened her womb; but Rachel was barren.

Leah conceived and bore a son, and she named him Reuben; for she said, 'Because the Lord has looked on my affliction; surely now my husband will love me.'

GENESIS 29:31-32

REUBEN

See, a son!

Yahweh has seen my unloved heart's affliction:
See, Jacob see – here is your first-born son,
REUBEN his name, born in my dereliction:
Yahweh has seen my unloved heart's affliction,
Given our union this fruitful benediction:
Richly our married life has now begun.
Yahweh has seen my unloved heart's affliction:
See, Jacob see – here is your first-born son.

Leah conceived again and bore a son, and said, 'Because the Lord has heard that I am hated, he has given me this son also'; and she named him Simeon.

SIMEON

I am heard

Yahweh has heard my unloved heart's complaining:
Hear, Jacob, hear the voice of your second son,
SIMEON his name: his piercing cry proclaiming
Yahweh has heard my unloved heart's complaining:
Through tiny lips and healthy lungs acclaiming
My hard-fought battle for your love is won.
Yahweh has heard my unloved heart's complaining.
Hear, Jacob, hear the voice of your second son.

Again Leah conceived and bore a son, and said, 'Now this time my husband will be joined to me, because I have borne him three sons'; therefore he was named Levi.

GENESIS 29:34

LEVI

Held and united

Yahweh has healed my aching soul's distress.
Hold in your arms this pledge of consolation
LEVI his name, cheeks smooth to soft caress:
Yahweh has healed my aching soul's distress:
Your strong embrace has sealed my happiness,
Ended long bitter years of cruel isolation.
Yahweh has healed my aching soul's distress.
Hold in your arms this pledge of consolation.

When Rachel saw that she bore Jacob no children, she envied her sister; and she said to Jacob, 'Give me children, or I shall die!'

Jacob became very angry with Rachel and said, 'Am I in the place of God, who has withheld from you the fruit of the womb?'

Then she said, 'Here is my maid Bilhah; go in to her, that she may bear upon my knees and that I too may have children through her.'

So she gave him her maid Bilhah as a wife; and Jacob went in to her.

And Bilhah conceived and bore Jacob a son.

Then Rachel said, 'God has judged me, and has also heard my voice and given me a son'; therefore she named him Dan (Justice).

GENESIS 30:1-6

SURROGATE BIRTH

Rachel's despairing cry:
'Give me children –
Give me children, or else
I die!'

Jacob's reply:
'God's surrogate?
Taking his place?
I?

But just as you please!'
At her persistent insistence
Prompt delivery
At her ease.

From the womb's door on to her knees –
Tiny limbs flailing,
Healthy lungs
Wailing.

'Dan is his name', she cries:
'Justice has been done:
God has given me
A son!'

But had he? Fatherhood
That silk-soft skin, smooth texture of small crumpled face
Left no doubt
About:

But motherhood ?
As for God, so for mother:
No surrogate:
No other.

'What shall I give you?' Laban asked. 'Don't give me anything,' Jacob replied. 'But if you will do this one thing for me, I will go on tending your flocks and watching over them:

Let me go through all your flocks today and remove from them every speckled or spotted sheep, every dark-coloured lamb and every spotted or speckled goat. They will be my wages.'

Jacob, however, took fresh-cut branches from poplar, almond and plane trees and made white stripes on them by peeling the bark and exposing the white inner wood of the branches.

Then he placed the peeled branches in all the watering troughs, so that they would be directly in front of the flocks when they came to drink. When the flocks were in heat and came to drink, they mated in front of the branches. And they bore young that were streaked or speckled or spotted.

In this way the man grew exceedingly prosperous and came to own large flocks, and maidservants and menservants, and camels and donkeys.

GENESIS 30:31-32,37-39,43

GENETIC ENGINEERING

Cunningly pilling white strakes
On rods of green poplar, hazel, chestnut:
Forming patterned fences beside the gutters,
He engineered the generation of a family fortune:

Controlled conception of speckled spotted cattle,
Ring-straked goats, brown among the sheep:
Fulfilment of his father's birth-right blessing
'Dew of heaven, fatness of earth, plenty of corn and wine'.

Gazing through mottled camouflage of screens of green
                                        and white,
On sweeping golden dunes of sand sprinkled with tufts of
                                        desert pasture,
He watched the flocks and herds acquire characteristics
Needed for his inheritance.

During wheat harvest, Reuben went out into the fields and found some mandrake plants, which he brought to his mother Leah. Rachel said to Leah, 'Please give me some of your son's mandrakes.'

But she said to her, 'Wasn't it enough that you took away my husband? Will you take my son's mandrakes too?' 'Very well,' Rachel said, 'he can sleep with you tonight in return for your son's mandrakes.'

So when Jacob came in from the fields that evening, Leah went out to meet him. 'You must sleep with me,' she said. 'I have hired you with my son's mandrakes.' So he slept with her that night.

GENESIS 30:14-16

Go and catch a falling star,
Get with child a mandrake root,
Tell me where all past years are,
Or who cleft the devil's foot.

JOHN DONNE – SONG

Mandrake: Forms large rosettes of flattened wrinkled leaves arising from a stout forked root. Fruits orange or yellow, like miniature tomatoes. Two closely related species: one with greenish yellow flowers appearing in the spring; the other with violet flowers found in the spring or autumn. Nightshade family.

POLUNIN – FLOWERS OF EUROPE

Mandrake: n. The narcotic and emetic herb Mandragora Autumnalis, used in magic and said to shriek when torn from the ground.

ODHAMS DICTIONARY

MANDRAKE

Leah –
Seeing only the image of innocence;
Six-year-old Reuben
Clutching at falling stars of violet flowers
Holding unfolding crinkled leaves of palest green,
Yielding and shielding globes of forming fruit
Born in the ripening corn.

But Rachel –
Seeing split root,
Aphrodisiac;
In night's deadly shade
Subtly narcotic,
Suggestively erotic:
Like twining naked legs
Torn from their bed,
Protesting, it is said,
With shrill cry,
At crude, rude disturbance
Of their privacy.

Was the price,
Like the star in the sky,
Too high?
The stratagem too wild?
One night
Alone,
Dreaming of gleaming mandrake root
Cleft like the devil's foot,
Getting with child?

And Jacob was left alone; and there wrestled with him a man until the breaking of the day.

And when he saw that he prevailed not against him, he touched the hollow of his thigh; and the hollow of Jacob's thigh was out of joint, as he wrestled with him.

And he said, 'Let me go, for the day breaketh.' And he said, 'I will not let thee go, except thou bless me.'

And he said, 'What is thy name?' And he said, 'Jacob'.

And he said, 'Thy name shall be called no more Jacob, but Israel: for as a prince hast thou power with God and with men, and hast prevailed'.

And Jacob asked him and said, 'Tell me, I pray thee, thy name'. And he said, 'Wherefore is it that thou dost ask after my name?' And he blessed him there.

And Jacob called the name of the place Peniel: for I have seen God face to face, and my life is preserved.

And as he passed over Peniel the sun rose upon him, and he halted upon his thigh.

GENESIS 32:24-31

DARK NIGHT

This fear again: utterly alone
As score years past last he fled,
Made in wild night pillow of pillar of stone
For his head: roughness of wind-swept turf for bed
Banished from carpeted comfort, domestic affection,
Gods-of-the-household's sheltering protection,
Physically, mentally, mystically out on his own:

But this time struggling, writhing,
Fearfully flinching from fury of attack:
In savage, bitter conflict driving
The cruel assassin flat upon his back:
Battling in vain, again, again
To wrest disclosure of the secret, sacred name: attain
Glorious triumphant end to cruel striving.

With sudden painful shock he felt the adversary displace
The hollow of his thigh: heard a voice proclaim, 'Israel,
Not Jacob is your name,' – glimpsing a face –
'God's powerful prince, with man you shall prevail'.
Defeated, dazed, halting on hollow thigh,
The sun rose on him, in the unclouded desert sky:
He gave a cry 'Peniel! God's face! How lovely is this place.'

Then they journeyed from Bethel; and when they were still some distance from Ephrath, Rachel was in childbirth, and she had hard labour.

When she was in her hard labour, the midwife said to her, 'Do not be afraid; for now you will have another son.'

As her soul was departing (for she died), she named him Ben-oni; but his father called him Benjamin.

So Rachel died, and she was buried on the way to Ephrath (that is, Bethlehem) and Jacob set up a pillar at her grave; it is the pillar of Rachel's tomb, which is there to this day.

GENESIS 35:16-20

For when I came from Paddan, Rachel, alas, died in the land of Canaan on the way, while there was still some distance to go to Ephrath; and I buried her there on the way to Ephrath (that is, Bethlehem).

GENESIS 48:7

NOT FAR FROM BETHLEHEM

It was here
On the Ephrath road
I buried Rachel.

Shepherdess by the well-side
Time for folding of sheep not come
Sun still high
In western sky.

Rachel
Beautiful and lovely
Not only in her name God's grace
But in the subtle changing softness
Of her face.

Giving the formal kiss of greeting
Relief delight
God's promise to me kept
I wept.

Joy persisted
Seemed but a day
Seven long years of toil unceasing
So great so glorious our love
Increasing.

Here was born
Her second child
Benoni she called him
Son of her desolation
Benjamin I named him
Son of my consolation.

Here on the Ephrath road
Not far from Bethlehem.

I buried Rachel.

Then Jacob gave them these instructions: 'I am about to be gathered to my people. Bury me with my fathers in the cave in the field of Ephron the Hittite, the cave in the field of Machpelah, near Mamre in Canaan, which Abraham bought as a burial place from Ephron the Hittite, along with the field. There Abraham and his wife Sarah were buried, there Isaac and his wife Rebekah were buried, and there I buried Leah.'

GENESIS 49:29-31

REQUIESCAT IN PACE

For the joy of loving
And living
There could be no one like Rachel
I fear.

But when it comes to dying,
I should prefer lying
Not by the pillar of Ephrath,
But in the cave of Machpelah:
With Abraham, Sarah, Isaac, Rebekah,

And Leah.

Credo

The fool hath said in his heart: there is no God.
The Lord looked down from heaven upon the children of men: to
see if there were any that would understand, and seek after God.

PSALMS 14:1,3

CREDO

I do not believe
There is
A God.
Among all the objects in
Or aspects of
The universe,
Why single this one out?
'This is a tree:
This is a pond:
This is a logarithm:
This is a nebula:
But this one is
A God.'

I do not believe
There is
A God.

I do not believe
A God
Exists:
Standing outside the rest,
Apart, beyond.

Yuri Gagarin went outside
His measured world
And cried
'There's no one there!'
And had he gone
Beyond the edge of space,
At journey's end
He would have nothing
        to declare
But: 'There is
No body,
Nobody,
No thing,
Nothing
There.'

I do not believe
A God
Exists.

But I am here:
So is the world of things
        and people
In all its beauty,
        all its terror:
So are the thoughts,
        hopes, dreams, and fears
Flooding from other minds
        to mine:
Bewildering inheritance
        of loveliness
And ugliness.

Confronted by
The mystery of Being,
Standing under
All that is,
I do not
Under-stand:
Not understanding
I am over-awed:
Being becomes Holy-Being.

I do not believe
There is a God:
I do not believe
A God
Exists:

But I believe
In God.

71

So the other disciples told him, 'We have seen the Lord.' But Thomas said to them, 'Unless I see the mark of the nails in his hands, and put my finger in the mark of the nails and my hand in his side, I will not believe.'

JOHN 20:25

Then they told what had happened on the road, and how he had been made known to them in the breaking of the bread.

LUKE 24:35

CRUST

Determined doubt, offspring of integrity,
Ruthlessly dissecting, fearlessly rejecting
Over-simplification's deadly implications –
Surrendering to scientific vision beatific:

The hard dry surface of a proposition,
Confusing complexity, bewildering perplexity –
Crumbling under pressure of persistent insistence
To subtle resolution, satisfying succulent solution:

Shyness, reserve, suspicion,
Mutual resistance to friendly co-existence –
Yielding like crust
To compassion, confidence, trust:

The breaking of the bread.

Truly, you are a God who hides himself.

ISAIAH 45:15

Revelation

We look for him in the wrong
Places, expecting to find him in the
Q.E.D. at the theorem's
Conclusion: reach out numbed
Hands to touch him in the
Smooth petals of flowering creation:
Peer blindly through long
Telescopes of technological and philosophical
Preception at bewildering
Nebulae or black holes of inter-stellar
Space. Yet perversely, like the hollow
Emptiness of the crisp
Footprint, the unimaginable
Density of the bright star's dark
Twin conceals what it reveals.

Out of the depths I cry to you, O Lord.

PSALMS 130:1

'Lord,' Martha said to Jesus, 'if you had been here, my brother would not have died.'

JOHN 11:21

Jesus wept.

JOHN 11: 35

THE SHAKING BED

I didn't know it was like that
Death agony was just a puzzling phrase
Drowned in the sound of angel trumpets
As pilgrim crossed the river to some promised land.

But now hour after hour the knobs of brass above my head
Shivered and rattled through the sleepless night
And not a sob or tear
No word said
Scarcely a prayer
As lying there in misery and dread
Turning from side to side
I tried in vain to stop this endless shaking
While thoughts and fears and doubts but never tears
Chased round and round my head in endless evil circle
And brass knobs trembled on the old iron bed.

And the next day the image of the eagle
Terror of beauty of those outspread golden wings
Swooping to destruction
As there we sat at school
Watching the speaker keeper demonstrate his skill
Harnessing aggression of his bird of prey
Equipped and swift to kill.

But in my mind picture of my loved sister
Battling with pain her swollen body utterly disfigured
Courage and kindness still persisting
Death fiercely resisting

And in my ears that tearing grating sound
Fight of young lungs for right to life
Then longer longer silence watching waiting
Through seeming endless night of misery and fright
And later dreadful unfeeling emptiness
No tears
No faith or hope to batten down my fears.

And in my head
The endless rattling of the shaking bed.

He makes springs pour water into the ravines; it flows between the mountains.

When you hide your face, they are terrified; when you take away their breath, they die and return to the dust.

When you send your Spirit, they are created, and you renew the face of the earth.

PSALMS 104:10, 29, 30

Jesus said to her, 'I am the resurrection and the life.'

JOHN 11:25

Therefore let us keep the Festival . . . with bread without yeast, the bread of sincerity and truth.

1 CORINTHIANS 5:8

THE GRAVE

*John Robinson, Bishop, is buried in the churchyard
at Arncliffe, North Yorkshire.*

Gleam of stream
Clean above green of mountain pasture
Now for a few yards buried in limestone soil,
Springing to life again in pool
Lucent as any lens,
Quivering with frogs:
Wedge-shaped bodies, bulging throats, protruding eyes,
Scissor-blade limbs with lithe smooth strokes
Slicing the water.

The river Skirfare
Emerging from hidden labyrinths
Swirling, splashing towards the Wharfe:
And on its banks
Warm marsh-marigold, cool primrose,
Sombre green and grey of leaves of winter snow-drop.

Squat solidity of church tower's perpendicularity,
Patched through centuries
With camouflage of white and orange lichen,
Matched by long dry-stone walls
Stretched taut across the fells.

The grave all of one piece with the dale:
The same simplicity, austerity, severity:
The same rough-pitted texture of limestone pavement
High in the hills where mountain turf
Spattered with wild yellow pansy
Gives place to Pennine millstone teeth
Biting pale northern skies with sharp precision.

Honest to God.

At that moment the curtain of the temple was torn in two, from top to bottom. The earth shook, and the rocks were split. The tombs also were opened and many bodies of the saints who had fallen asleep were raised. After his resurrection they came out of the tombs and entered the holy city and appeared to many.

MATTHEW 27: 51-53

And the one who was seated on the throne said, 'See, I am making all things new.'

REVELATION 21:5

PIED PIPER

Alive
Not just in memory
Not in some other world than this if such there be
But in this world's totality.

The chip-chip-chopping of the axe of pre-historic man
Echoes, resounds around today's technology.

Splash of one pebble in this present pool
Creates expanding circles spreading to infinity.

Doors to the past not bolted barred
But flung wide open to eternity.

Touch of the moment
Sudden smile or glance
Flash of humour
Sadness of a sigh
Cry of delight of wonder or of pain
Are not just here today and gone and that forever's that
But there
Painted indelibly the light the shade
In subtle patterned perpetuity.

As yesterday's so is today's
World without end.

Pied Piper Christ
Wearing the motley of our hopes and fears
Bearing our joys and sins
Split open all our graves.

Lead from the jaws of hell the present and the past
The not-yet-born the living and the dead.

Make all things new.

Then the Lord answered Job out of the whirlwind:

'Who is this that darkens counsel by words without knowledge?

Gird up your loins like a man, I will question you, and you shall declare to me.

Where were you when I laid the foundation of the earth? Tell me, if you have understanding.

Who determined its measurements – surely you know! Or who stretched the line upon it?

When the morning stars sang together and all the heavenly beings shouted for joy?'

JOB 38:1-5, 7

Marking time

What was the time
When time began?
Who made time, found time, lost time
Before man?

What was a year
Before the earth went round the sun?
How long a day
Before it spun?

Tell me if you can
Where newly made space
Was found a place
When at that first Great Bang
Morning stars sang?

Is time a straight line?
No other dimension:
Just limit-less extension?
Or does it at life's end –
The world's or mine –
Take a sharp bend
And turn into
Eternity?

'For in him we live and move and have our being.' As some of your own poets have said, 'We are his offspring.'

ACTS 17:28

'I am the Alpha and the Omega, the First and the Last, the Beginning and the End.'

REVELATION 22:13

GOD OUT THERE

Why must I always stay within?
Can't I go out to play?
Leap from your inner world of shades
Into the light of day?

Am I the prisoner of your thoughts?
Why won't you set me free?
The world without is my within
And your within is me.

I am the ground from which you spring,
Your over-arching sky.
Subject and object I am both:
The great I AM am I.

From noon on, darkness came over the whole land until three in the afternoon. And about three o'clock Jesus cried with a loud voice. 'Eli, Eli, lama sabachthani?' that is, 'My God, my God, why have you forsaken me?'

MATTHEW 27:45-46

TE DEUM

Incongruous images grotesquely inter-twined:
Terrors of delusion the reeling mind resists:
The slide into confusion: facing with clenched fists
Phantasies of horror: helpless, hopeless, blind.

Confounded, bewildered, twisted, tortured mind:
Eyes vainly scouring dark encroaching mists –
Yet, through confusion, clarity of voice persists,
Piercing deaf's darkness with vowels sharp, defined.

So, when I slide into the jaws of hell,
Back to primeval chaos, before the first creation,
The cry that over Golgotha resounded,
In sharpest tones of clear enunciation,
'My God, my God!' – may be my cry as well.
Trusting in you, let me never be confounded.

And now faith, hope and love abide, these three: and the greatest of these is love.

1 CORINTHIANS 13:13

Pursue love and strive for the spiritual gifts.

1 CORINTHIANS 14:1

THE SPINNING SPECTRUM

Faith:
Not clinging on in desperation
Or exasperation:
But despite perplexity
Saying 'Yes' to creation
In all its complexity.

Hope:
Not kidding yourself,
But deliberately ridding yourself
Of gloomy prognostications:
Spotting the best intimations
In the worst situations.

Love:
Spinning the totality
Of the whole spectrum of morality –
Gentleness, meekness, kindness and peace mixed
Inextricably with faith and hope – fixed
In the blinding clarity
And sublime hilarity
Of charity.

In that region there were shepherds living in the fields, keeping watch over their flock by night. Then an angel of the Lord stood before them, and the glory of the Lord shone around them, and they were terrified. But the angel said to them. 'Do not be afraid; for see – I am bringing you good news of great joy for all the people: to you is born this day in the city of David a Saviour, who is the Messiah, the Lord. This will be a sign for you: you will find a child wrapped in bands of cloth and lying in a manger.'

LUKE 2:8-12

Let the same mind be in you that was in Christ Jesus, who, though he was in the form of God, did not regard equality with God as something to be exploited, but emptied himself, taking the form of a slave, being born in human likeness. And being found in human form, he humbled himself and became obedient to the point of death – even death on a cross. Therefore God also highly exalted him and gave him the name that is above every name, so that at the name of Jesus every knee should bend, in heaven and under the earth, and every tongue confess that Jesus Christ is Lord, to the glory of God the Father.

PHILIPPIANS 2:5-11

KENOSIS

Equality with godhead outpoured overnight!
How could the Lord and Master of us all
Become so small
And in this rough deserted place
Emptied of glory, majesty and might
Be born the child of Mary, full of grace
And at her breast
Find rest?

Leaving his heavenly throne at God's right hand on high,
Clothed in humility, child of the stable,
How was he able
To learn obedience, endure our loss,
Share our humanity, suffer and die,
That we, rejoicing in his glorious cross
May evermore acclaim
His holy Name.

RELATIVITY

Height length and breadth –
Without the other
Two of the three
Reduce space to a plan
Or two contrasted elevations:
Partiality lacking proportion,
Visual distortion.

Past present future –
Without the other
Two of the three
Reduce time to history
Mythology or prophecy:
Reality's contortion,
Eternity's abortion.

Space without time
Has no persistance:
Time without space
No existence:
Six counter-tensioned strands –
One inter-woven cable?
Unbelievable? Inconceivable?

But glimpse this vision:
Time is not spaceless,
Space not timeless:
Within the womb of each
The other lies:
Reality's mystical maternity,
Immaculate conception of eternity.